GREAT BUSINESS STORIES

# ANITA RODDICK AND THE BODY SHOP

PAUL BROWN

**OTHER TITLES IN THE SERIES**

Akio Morita and Sony by David Marshall
Coco Chanel and Chanel by David Bond
Bill Gates and Microsoft by David Marshall
George Eastman and Kodak by Peter Brooke-Ball
Henry Ford and Ford by Michael Pollard

**Picture Credits**

Exley Publications is grateful to the following individuals and organizations for permission to reproduce their pictures. Whilst every effort has been made to trace copyright holders, we would be happy to hear from any not here acknowledged.

**Environmental Picture Library:** 31-32/Steve Morgan; **Images Colour Library:** 44/Andris Apse; **Popperfoto:** 28/Johnny Eggitt, 29; **Rex Features:** 4, 5/Today, 9 (bottom)/Tony White, 25/TIM, 33/Tom Kidd, 39 (top); **The Body Shop Picture Library:** 6, 7 (both), 8, 9 (top), 10/Antonio Vizcaino, 11, 12, 13, (top)/Clive Boursnell, 13 (bottom), 15, 17, 18, 19, 20 (both), 21 (all), 22 (both), 23, 24 (both), 26/Clive Boursnell, 27, 34 (all), 35, 36, 37, 38/Clive Boursnell, 39 (bottom), 40 (both), 41, 42, 43, 45/Thomas Kelly, 47 (top)/Carol Beckwith, 47 (bottom)/Antonio Vizcaino, 49 (top)/Carol Beckwith, 50 (top)/Carol Beckwith, 50 (bottom)/Thomas Kelly, 52 (top)/Clive Boursnell, 52 (bottom), 53, 55/Derek Martin, 56/Ian Cook, 59, 60.

Published in Great Britain in 1996
by Exley Publications Ltd,
16 Chalk Hill, Watford,
Herts WD1 4BN, United Kingdom.



**A copy of the CIP data is available from the British Library on request.**

**ISBN 1-85015-481-3**



**Series editor: Samantha Armstrong**
Editorial assistants: Kathryn & David Marshall, Helen Lanz
Picture editors: Alex Goldberg and James Clift
of Image Select
Typeset by Delta Print, Watford, Herts, U.K.
Printed in Dubai

# ANITA RODDICK AND THE BODY SHOP

PAUL BROWN

EXLEY
NEW YORK • WATFORD, UK

*Opposite: The founder of The Body Shop, Anita Roddick. A spokesperson of the Confederation of British Industry (CBI) has said . . . "The most successful business women – like Anita Roddick – have tended to follow their own noses rather than take more traditional business routes."*

*Below: Anita demonstrating against the destruction of the Amazon rainforest. From the start, Anita used the influence of The Body Shop to campaign for environmental and social issues.*

## A totally new kind of product

It was 1976 and shopkeepers in Brighton, on the south coast of England, wondered what the strange woman with messy hair was doing spraying strawberry essence everywhere. Anita Roddick was laying a scent trail to attract customers to her latest business, The Body Shop. "Believe me, I was prepared to try anything in those early days to get customers into my shop," she remembered. It was just one of her many ideas that brought in the public.

Anita Roddick, aged thirty-four, had decided on a completely new kind of business, selling totally new products. She would create beauty products out of ingredients like coconut oil and rosewater, and avocado, she would sell them in quantities people wanted to buy and neither the products nor their ingredients would be animal tested on her behalf. She was opposed to testing cosmetics on animals.

## Business and principles

Right from the outset, Anita decided that she would strive to combine running a business with upholding certain ethical values in which she believed. The principle of not testing products or ingredients on animals was one of her beliefs, and one she felt she shared with many potential customers. She also made it her policy to ensure that natural ingredients were used. Initially, recycling was through necessity – Anita couldn't afford to buy in new bottles so had to encourage her customers to bring their old ones back for a refill.

*Rows of products line the shelves of one of the first Body Shops. Long before recycling became fashionable, Anita was encouraging customers to have their empty containers refilled.*
*Opposite top: Anita Roddick always wanted her customers to feel good about themselves. These are not fashion models, but Body Shop employees.*
*Opposite bottom: Anita was never scared to get her hands dirty!*

Gradually, this idea was developed into a deliberate policy, with conservation in mind. By 1994, 73% of The Body Shop's main products used fully recyclable packaging and 13% carried no packaging at all. The effort to avoid waste became more and more a part of The Body Shop's overall business doctrine as the company expanded. Similarly, concern for the environment led on to another central policy – concern for people. This extended from care for employees, as the company grew, to caring for the cultural and economic welfare of the communities from which The Body Shop was buying an increasing proportion of its raw materials. With over 1,300 outlets in more than forty-five countries by 1995, The Body Shop seemed an obvious idea.

In the early seventies, however, the cosmetics business was very different and it made Anita

Roddick angry. Perfumes, skin creams, shampoos, and other cosmetics were sold in large jars and containers. They traded, she felt, on women's insecurities about their bodies, selling products at high prices along with promises of everlasting youth and exquisite beauty.

"It is immoral to trade on fear. It is immoral constantly to make women feel dissatisfied with their bodies. It is immoral to deceive a customer by making miracle claims for a product," she said. Anita also reasoned that if chocolates and cheese could be sold in small amounts why not cosmetics. Why not put them in cheap containers with honest labels describing their benefits?

But in 1976, although she never put her ideals on one side, Anita's first priority was to make The Body Shop succeed. With two children to care for and with a shared ambition for her husband, Gordon, to go to South America to carry out a childhood ambition to travel through the continent on horseback, Anita Roddick had to make some money.

*Big is not always beautiful!*

*Opposite top: The eye-catching green of The Body Shop is instantly recognizable all over the world.*

## Getting started

Being angry about the beauty trade, having energy, a good idea, and a reason to make the business work was not enough. In order to rent and decorate premises, and buy products to sell, Anita needed a loan. She went to her appointment with the bank manager dressed in jeans and a T-shirt with a pop star on the front, and carrying her children.

It was partly the scruffy appearance that meant Anita Roddick's request for a loan was denied. But also, the bank felt that lending money to a woman with a "crazy" business idea and two children was not a risk it wanted to take.

Anita did not have a business plan. When people lend money, whether a bank or an individual, they want to know when they can expect to get it back. A business plan outlines the expected costs of setting up a business, advertising, printing headed paper, and sets forward the proposed sales figures for a month, two months, six months, and so on. As soon as the money coming in from sales is greater than the costs of running the business, the business is making a profit. Money from that profit can then be put toward paying back the loan. Banks, however, do not lend money just on a good business plan, they also require collateral. Collateral is the term given to something valuable which, if the business fails, the bank can have in exchange for its money.

After the first disappointment of being denied a loan, Anita took advice from her husband. She prepared a business plan and when the day came for her second appointment, she dressed appropriately. Gordon also went with her to the meeting. Whether it was the clothes, the business plan or the presence of a man, the loan was granted. Collateral was provided in the shape of their previous business venture and family home, St. Winifred's Hotel.

## Supplies needed

The next step was to locate suppliers of the natural ingredients Anita wanted to use. Cosmetic manufacturers were not interested in supplying The

Body Shop not only because of the small amounts required, but also because they were not familiar with the ingredients requested. A young herbalist, Mark Constantine, however, was. A list of twenty-five products was agreed upon to launch the product range. Some had natural ingredients like almond oil and cocoa butter.

Anita's home town, Littlehampton, on the south coast of England, was too small and traditional for her revolutionary idea. So Anita turned to somewhere much larger, more fashionable, and with a strong student and artistic culture in which to locate her first outlet – Brighton.

The premises were in a good position in a pedestrian precinct. However, the interior was dingy, damp was running down the walls, and there was a healthy growth of green fungi. To hide the fungi, Anita picked an identical shade of green paint and hung the walls with garden trellis.

*Anita with her husband and business partner, Gordon.*

*"From the beginning, The Body Shop was about communication between shops and customers."*

*"My mother once said I ran my shop the way she ran her household during the Second World War. Then, she wasn't being environmental. She was simply a good housekeeper. I was doing the same. And it worked. Common sense usually does."*

*Anita Roddick, from* The Body Shop Book.

*Ingredients for The Body Shop products come from all over the world.*

The shelves looked pretty empty with only twenty-five different products on them. So, using the cheapest containers possible – urine sample bottles – five different sizes of each product were stacked on the shelves. Now people could buy exactly how much or how little they wanted.

To keep costs down even further, a promotion advised people to bring back their empty containers to get them refilled at a discount. Not only did this bring customers back into the shop again, but it started recycling – at this stage as a money saving idea, rather than out of concern for the environment. It was a totally new concept in the 1970s.

## Body trouble

Anita proudly painted the name The Body Shop over her new business. To her amazement, she got a letter from two local undertakers who were trying to prevent her using the name. They said "The Body Shop" would interfere with the funeral business.

Anita Roddick immediately reacted with some of the entrepreneurial skill for which she later became known. Instead of being bullied by the letter, she gave the story to the local newspaper – a gang of undertakers was trying to stop a poor, harmless woman from opening her own business, while her husband was planning to go off and ride a horse across South America!

The resulting publicity had a double effect. The undertakers did not follow it up and, when the shop opened, there were crowds of people wanting to have a look at this new and exciting place.

By 12:00 p.m. Anita was so busy she telephoned Gordon to come and help. By 6:00 p.m. they had taken £130. They had set the weekly target at £300 to keep the business going. "I was not just happy," she said. "I was euphoric."

## Learning by experience

Part of Anita Roddick's teething problems, but also one of the main reasons for her success, was that she knew nothing about traditional business practices and so created a distinct style of her own. "I probably wouldn't have succeeded had I been taught about business," she recalled.

She knew, however, that although the first day had been a success, the customers had to keep coming back. As well as her ploy of spraying the street with strawberry essence, she put large posters and sandwich boards outside the premises promoting the products to make people take notice.

Inside, the atmosphere was different from other places where the assistants would be on one side of the counter and the customers on the other. Instead, Anita mingled with the customers and what really made Anita different from most shopkeepers was her enthusiasm. "Talking about the products was never a chore," she recalled. "Passion persuades and by God I was passionate about what I was selling."

She set up a little perfume bar with a selection of perfume oils such as apple blossom, jasmine and honeysuckle, so customers could choose fragrances and match them to their other purchases. "Mmm, I love the smell of this," Anita would say. "Here, try it. What do you think?"

*The Body Shop's R&D team test all their products. In the early days, Anita experimented in her kitchen with ingredients.*

## Natural ingredients

She had a new kind of product with strange ingredients, many of them from exotic parts of the world, such as Tahiti, where Anita had visited on her travels. She was selling Honey and Oatmeal Scrub Mask, Cucumber Cleansing Milk, Seaweed and Birch Shampoo, Avocado Moisture Cream, and Cocoa Butter Body Lotion – all of which needed some explaining to most of the customers.

She was able to tell them how, in Tahiti, in the South Pacific, she had seen Polynesian women with soft, beautiful skin. In such a hot climate, skin would tend to dry up and wrinkle yet their skins were smooth and supple – there had to be a secret ingredient. It was a substance that looked like lumps of cooking fat. It was cocoa butter made from cocoa pods and the women rubbed it into their skin to retain its natural moisture. Anita tried it herself.

***"Women are much better at starting up businesses because they tend to go into areas where there's a proven need that they've recognized or needed themselves. Men tend to want to go into small-scale reproductions of big businesses."***

*Rob Donnelly, Head of Manpower and Employee Relations at the CBI.*

In other parts of the world she found women using other methods to care for their skins and bodies without using any modern cosmetics. They were using natural ingredients, the knowledge of which had been passed down through generations.

## Simply hard work

In the evenings, Anita Roddick experimented with various ingredients to try to make existing products better and to create new ones.

Unable to afford help, all the bottling had to be done in a room at the back of the premises. The products came in five gallon containers and had to be poured into hundreds of smaller ones – a hard physical job after a day serving customers. To increase the takings of the business, The Body Shop opened on Sundays as well. The two children, now seven and six, stayed with Anita's mother. "I could never have coped in those early days if it had not been for my mother," Anita remembered.

Along with Anita's enthusiasm and need to make money, the business needed a boost to launch it firmly on its feet. The boost came when the summer of 1976 was one of Britain's hottest. The long, dry spell brought visitors from London to the sea at Brighton.

People coming to the beach were exposing more and more flesh as one sunny day followed another. To protect their skin and improve their tans, they began to use more and more of The Body Shop skin products.

Just six months after opening, the business was making a profit. Already Anita Roddick wanted to start expanding it.

***"For us beauty is a healthy part of everyday life. It's all about character and curiosity and imagination and humour - in short it's an active outward expression of everything you like about yourself."***

*Rosemary Lomax, from the* Watford Observer, January 20, 1995.

*The Perella sisters in 1945 - Anita (on the left), the youngest, Lydia and Velia.*

## Work ethic

Anita had seen a lot of the world by the time she opened the first branch of The Body Shop when she was thirty-four years old. She had been born Anita Perella in 1942 in Littlehampton. It was a typical English seaside resort, with people spending their long summer breaks there.

The Perellas were Italian immigrants and they owned a small café called The Clifton. Anita's mother, Gilda, did the cooking and her grandmother prepared food. Anita, with her two older sisters and younger brother, was pressed into service taking orders, clearing tables, washing the dishes, and buttering hundreds of slices of bread. "The work ethic, the idea of service, was second nature to us," Anita said.

When Anita was eight years old her parents divorced and Gilda married again. Her new husband was known to the children as Uncle Henry.

Henry had lived in the United States and he quickly changed the café into an American-style diner, with a long bar and high stools, pinball machines, and a jukebox. It brought people flocking in. Anita could see the benefits of marketing and changing the image of a place first hand.

## An eye for business

Uncle Henry had also brought a large quantity of comics and bubble gum back with him from the United States. Anita discovered that she could trade these much-prized commodities for whole collections of cigarette cards and picture albums.

Although the comics were all at home, Anita claimed they were arriving in small batches from the States. She had already learned that what was in short supply was valuable, so, by bringing them out weekly, she did not flood the market.

While she was still going to school, Anita also discovered that some people needed help and support and that she could give it. She swapped her brand new school uniform with another girl whose uniform was old and tattered and whose family could not afford a new one. The reaction of her mother was not so positive!

By the time Anita left school she wanted to become an actress. However, she decided that the teaching profession offered a more secure future and so she began teacher training.

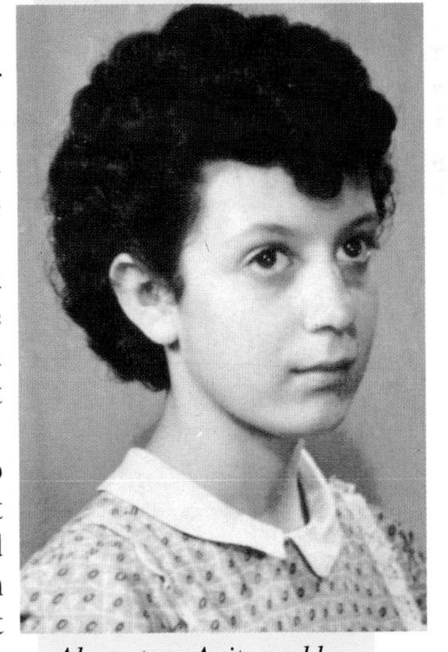

*Above top: Anita and her mother, Gilda. "Be special," Gilda said, "Be anything but mediocre." Above: Anita Perella, aged 10.*

## Paris

In 1962, when Anita was twenty, a scholarship sent her to Israel for three months where she worked in a communal work camp, a kibbutz, for a month. The remaining two months were spent learning how to travel alone.

England seemed dull by comparison and, on her return, she almost immediately went to Paris for a year, where she took a job in a newspaper library. Hitchhiking to Greece came next and then she went across to Switzerland where her enthusiasm persuaded the United Nations to give her a job.

By then a wanderlust had a deep hold on Anita and, with the savings of a year's work, she was off again. This time she went to the South Pacific and Tahiti, island hopping all the way to Australia.

After Australia, she went around the world to South Africa, where Anita Perella was arrested. Because of apartheid, the name given to the strict rules that were then in force in South Africa to keep the races apart, alternate nights at a local disco were designated for whites and blacks. Anita went to the night set aside for black people. She was given twenty-four hours to leave the country.

With just enough money for a ticket back to England, twenty-five-year-old Anita returned to Littlehampton. Even before she had time to tell her mother where she had been and what had happened Gilda told her that there was a man she had to meet. It was a meeting that was to change Anita's life.

## Love at first sight?

***"We'll compromise anything, just as long as it is not our values, or our aesthetics, or our ideals or our sense of curiosity, because they are the things that draw from the very core of our being."***

*Anita Roddick.*

From their first meeting, Anita decided that Gordon Roddick was the man for her. She was loud and brash and he was quiet and thoughtful, but they had a lot in common.

He had been around the world as much as she had. They shared many of the same values and the same hopes and dreams. Their politics were the same, they both campaigned for an end to the making and stockpiling of nuclear bombs. Within a week, Anita and Gordon had moved in together and plans to go overland to Australia to start a pineapple plantation were in the air. Then Anita became pregnant which put an end to that idea. In August 1969, Justine Roddick was born.

Anita and Gordon married in 1970 and, in July 1971, a second baby girl, Samantha, was born. The Roddicks, after trying one or two trades, such as picture framing, decided they wanted a business they could run together, as a family.

*Anita with her second daughter, Samantha, in 1972. Fifteen years later, Samantha would travel with Anita to the Amazon rainforest and attend the Forest Peoples' Gathering.*

***"We never aimed to be in this position, and that protected us – not knowing how to run a business, never employing anyone who had been to a business school and saying very simple things, like why not? Why should I leave my values at home? Why can't I campaign for human rights? I do that normally, so why the hell can't I bring it in to work?"***

*Anita Roddick.*

## Going into business

The first joint venture was a hotel named St. Winifred's. The summer season of 1971 went well except that it was hard work looking after a family and cooking twenty breakfasts every morning. At the end of the season, however, there were no more guests and the bills piled up.

The couple had to adapt quickly to avoid running out of money or going bankrupt, so they turned part of the hotel into a residential home. Their next venture, with money borrowed with the hotel as collateral, was named Paddington's Restaurant. They began with an Italian style health food restaurant – it flopped. For three weeks they sat in an empty restaurant with no customers. What saved Anita and Gordon from bankruptcy was their ability to recognize they were wrong and move on quickly to the next idea. "We had done everything wrong. It was the wrong kind of restaurant in the wrong street in the wrong town, launched at the wrong time."

Adaptability in a new business, when some ideas work and some fail, is vital. To wait too long might be fatal. Thus the Italian health food restaurant was transformed into an American style hamburger joint. It became an overnight success.

## Birth of The Body Shop

Here a pattern emerged in their working relationship that would remain in place during The Body Shop years. The original intention was for Anita to do the cooking and for Gordon to be in the restaurant taking orders and dealing with the customers. After a couple of days, the kitchen was a mess and Gordon's direct manner was offending customers. To avert disaster, they swapped roles, Anita dealing with the customers and Gordon making sure the organization ran smoothly. It worked in the hamburger restaurant and it was to work in The Body Shop. Anita and Gordon's was a business partnership that made the most of each person's strengths, and made up for their weaknesses, too.

Three years of running a restaurant full-time and an hotel part-time, while bringing up a family, exhausted the couple. Despite their hard work, the Roddicks were not making much money. They decided to get out.

Once the restaurant was sold, Gordon wanted to carry out his childhood ambition to ride a horse from Buenos Aires in Argentina to New York in the United States. It was a dangerous trip of 5,300 miles, (8400 km) through most of South America, right along the length of Central America and across the United States.

While Gordon planned his trip, Anita came up with the idea of The Body Shop.

***"Beauty begins with fitness and well-being, and the earlier you start, the younger you'll look as you grow older."***

***"The time has come to redefine beauty and to question the cosmetics industry.... Beauty is personal and individual; it is also holistic. Taking care of your health and skin is far more important than trying to change a feature that doesn't quite match up to current trends."***

*From* The Body Shop Book.

## Expansion

After the first branch of The Body Shop had opened and the hot summer weather had brought high sales, Anita was keen to expand. The business had only been going a few months but, "Wouldn't it be great, wouldn't it be cheeky, if I could replicate the Brighton shop somewhere else?" Anita thought.

She had faith in her idea and wanted to see how far she could go. Anita discussed the possibility of opening a second outlet with a friend, Aidre, who worked in The Body Shop. The sensible approach would have been to build up the one store for a few years, but Anita was impulsive and impatient. "That is the difference between an entrepreneur and a non-entrepreneur.... Entrepreneurs are doers as well as dreamers – they want to find the best way of pushing an idea along and use money to oil the wheels." She chose her next location and immediately toured the town to find suitable premises.

She was ready to take the plunge into business number two. She went back to the bank to borrow another £4,000, but the manager told Anita to wait another year.

"I had to find someone willing to invest in me – someone who would realize I didn't do things by halves, that I had energy and a total commitment to what I was doing," Anita stated.

What she needed was a financial backer – someone who would have faith in her business idea and was prepared to invest some money to get it underway. They would then own part of the business and would benefit if it succeeded. If it failed, their money would be lost.

*Anita opened the second Body Shop in September 1976 – just six months after the first shop had opened. Her energy and total commitment to The Body Shop have enabled it to grow into a global company with outlets all over the world.*

## A good investment

Aidre's boyfriend, Ian McGlinn, a local garage owner, had some spare capital. He agreed to give Anita £4,000 for half the business. As far as Anita

> ***"I think the fashion and beauty industries miss every opportunity that is offered them to celebrate diversity .... What I would like to see is a redefinition of beauty from the beauty business, an endorsement of character and diversity rather than promotion of a physical ideal. I think it is much healthier to take a holistic view - to look at the whole body and soul."***
>
> *Anita Roddick.*

was concerned there was not much of a business to split, and besides, it was the only deal she could get, so she decided to go ahead. She wrote to Gordon and told him what she was going to do. By the time he wrote back to tell her not to sell half the business, it was too late.

For Ian McGlinn, the first shareholder in The Body Shop, it was the best investment he ever made. The £4,000 investment in 1976 was worth just under £100 million by 1996.

The second outlet opened in September 1976 with Aidre in charge. It was bigger than the original one and it was more difficult to fill the space with the limited number of products. As a result, it was decided to diversify.

Earrings, necklaces, bright scarves, cards, and books, anything they thought they could sell was put onto the shelves. The philosophy was that The Body

*Fruit salad for your lips! A selection of The Body Shop lip-balms in a range of luscious tastes.*

Shop was now fighting both for its survival and for its long term future prospects, so anything that was saleable was sold.

***"I probably wouldn't have succeeded had I been taught about business."***
*Anita Roddick.*

## Gut instinct

The day that both shops took £100, Anita said, "Nothing could dampen my excitement. I had never, ever, thought that we would be able to notch up such figures. It was wonderful to have such a positive indication that I had got it right, that I was right to trust my gut instinct, that we were providing products that people wanted and charging a price they were willing to pay and still enable us to make a profit. To me that was bliss."

***"Women are more creative in their thinking. They aren't usually traditionalists."***
*Anita Roddick.*

In 1977, after an absence of nearly a year, Gordon came home from his travels and immediately got involved with the business. He moved the whole bottling and label-making plant into the family garage and delivered supplies to both shops as needed. He took over paying the wages and doing the accounts for the business. His return gave new impetus to the business. He felt the way to expand, without having to borrow money or find a financial backer, was to create a franchise system.

## One big family

People had already come into the stores asking if they could open a branch of The Body Shop – they saw that it was doing well and could be a successful business venture with which to get involved. With a franchise system, they would be granted the right to open a branch of The Body Shop and stock its products. They would own or rent the premises themselves and spend money fitting it out. The Body Shop would provide the products. It meant more and more products could be sold.

By making products in bulk and supplying them to a number of premises, the cost of each individual item went down and therefore increased the potential profit for both the particular owner and the Roddicks. The Roddicks themselves used the outlets they owned to test the products and to see how well

*The Body Shop recycling campaign was launched in 1992. Every shop put up posters to encourage customers to recycle or refill their bottles. Targets were set for the number of bottles each store should try to collect each week.*

*Above and opposite: By the 1990s, The Body Shop range had come a long way from the original twenty-five products for sale in Anita's first shop. The range now included an almost mouth-watering array of shampoos, soaps and suntan lotion.*

each one sold. If they were popular, they would be distributed to the franchises.

In 1978, two years after The Body Shop premises in Brighton had opened, the first independently-owned branches began to appear. Gordon and Anita offered their expertise and experience in helping to start up the branches and how to run them. As often as not this meant getting their overalls on to prepare the premises for the opening day.

Their involvement with staff training and the direction of each branch was always close. This was in order that The Body Shop staff felt like part of one great family business wherever they worked and also so that no single branch of The Body Shop strayed away from the company image.

## Growing pains?

The Roddicks knew they had a success on their hands when one franchise holder phoned Gordon to ask him how to work a calculator. The Body Shop

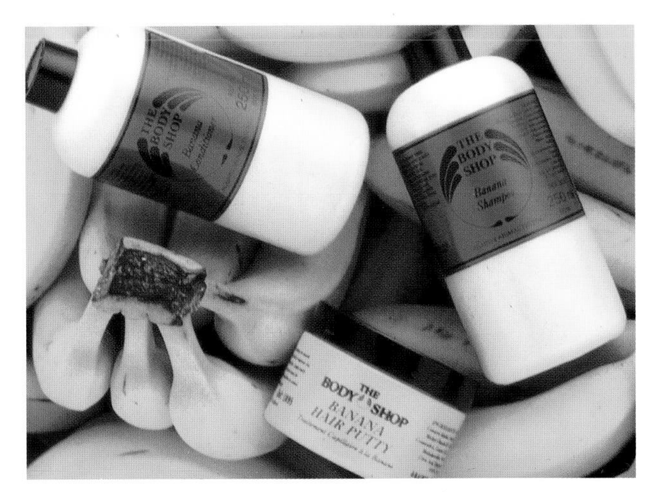
THE BODY SHOP
THE BODY SHOP
BANANA
HAIR PUTTY

THE BODY SHOP
Watermelon
SPF
THE BODY SHOP
SPF
THE BODY SHOP
SPF
SPF 20+
SPF 20+

environments in danger
THE BODY SHOP
THE BODY SHOP
forest jelly bath bubbles

was not about money, but about trade. Ten years later, that same franchise holder had five branches in Britain.

The Roddicks were also expanding the business themselves. The bank was, at last, growing in confidence and lent them enough money to open a third outlet. It was still a struggle. The little green van that Anita used repeatedly broke down, making it difficult to complete the two-hour journey to the store. The expansion meant the family garage was no longer adequate for bottling the products so Gordon moved the bottling plant into a large warehouse.

Despite this rapid growth, getting supplies was rarely a problem. Anita was unused to normal business practice where bills were settled six weeks or longer after goods were delivered. Instead she always paid at once. Suppliers were so delighted to be paid on delivery that Anita could always count on them to deliver on time.

Trading patterns, or the number of sales made, vary from one month to the next, for example during the summer or in the run-up to Christmas. One month's figures cannot always be compared with the month before to get a true picture of how the business is progressing. However, once the first year's trading was complete, it was possible to look at two months that were alike. Gordon was well satisfied with progress.

*The Body Shop went international in 1978 with the opening of the first franchise outside the UK. As these pictures show no matter where in the world – whether in Italy (above), Antigua (below) or Saudi Arabia (opposite) – The Body Shop is instantly recognizable.*

## Going international

From an early stage The Body Shop went international. The first overseas franchise was in a kiosk in Brussels. It was so small that the first order for stock was minimal. In 1979, Sweden's first branch of The Body Shop opened in Stockholm and one was started in Athens in Greece. Another opened in Canada. Eventually every country with branches of The Body Shop in it was run by one head franchise holder. "They are all individual entrepreneurs, all keen to be successful," Gordon reflected. The products they stocked, however, had to be adapted for the different international markets.

The BODY SHOP
الزينه والجمال

The BODY SHOP
Skin & Hair Care Preparations

*Peppermint Foot Lotion became one of The Body Shop's best sellers, thanks in part to Anita's unusual marketing tactic during the London Marathons of the early 1980s.*

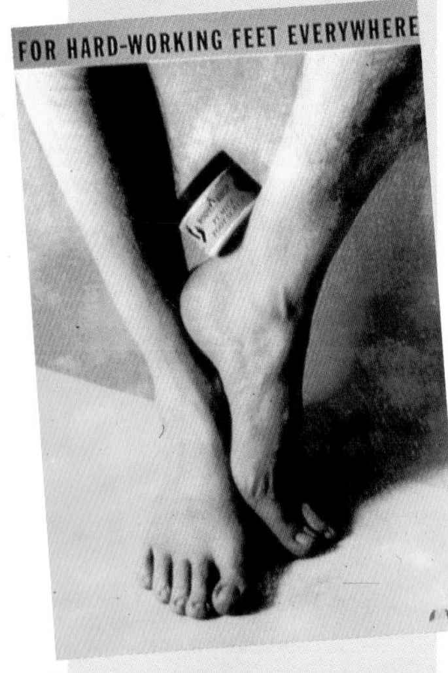


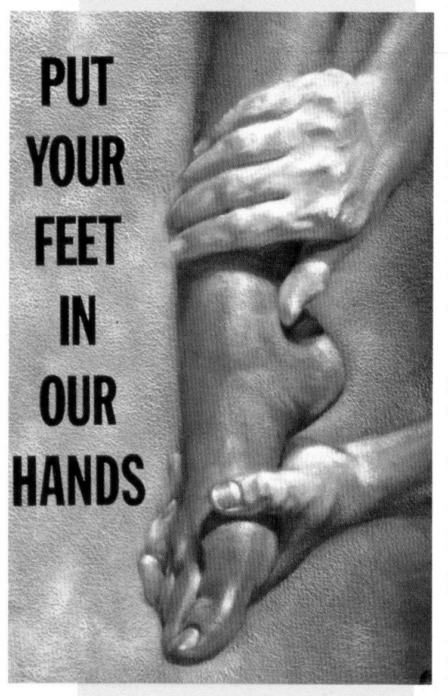


Although the first priority had to be the financial survival of the business, other characteristics of The Body Shop began to show themselves. The herbalist, Mark Constantine, began running short courses for the workforce. He taught employees about the products and about hair and skin care. The Body Shop philosophy was that everyone, including those working part-time, should know more about the products than any of the customers.

In order to try to learn more herself, Anita went to conferences and presentations given by the big cosmetic houses, like Revlon and Estée Lauder. They reinforced her beliefs that she did not like the industry with its expensive bottles and hype. While The Body Shop was telling people what was in its products, the rest of the cosmetics industry was relying on gimmicks such as "factor X."

## Smelly feet

Anita Roddick also objected to the way that other cosmetic companies advertised their products. She said the cosmetics industry peddled false dreams and downright lies. This could create unhappiness and insecurity among women, at whom the cosmetics were aimed, by suggesting that the use of their cosmetics would turn everyone into a model or movie star. Anita felt strongly that there was far more to the cosmetic trade than this, "For us at The Body Shop, beauty is a healthy part of everyday life. It's all about character and curiosity and imagination and humour – in short, it's an active outward expression of everything you like about yourself."

Another factor that annoyed Anita was that up to £5 million could be spent just launching one product. The cost of all this advertising was added to the cost of each jar of cosmetics so the customer paid for it. Anita's flair for free publicity convinced her that much advertising could be done creatively without great cost.

An example of this followed a marathon race in London. As one member of staff pointed out, The Body Shop did not stock a lotion for tired feet. Mark Constantine came up with one made from peppermint, menthol and arnica, with almond oil, cocoa butter, and lanolin. Apart from the soothing effect it had on tired feet, it also helped to stop them smelling. The bottles were handed out to the marathon runners as they went past. The papers picked up the story and Peppermint Foot Lotion became one of the best-selling lines.

## A different style of promotion

Anita capitalized on this alternative style of promoting her products. Through her stores she started to air her social and ethical concerns – making them a fundamental part of her approach to business. Anita spent time campaigning against testing cosmetics on animals, and on saving the whales. The publicity such campaigning attracted was effectively a form of free advertising, but Anita would have done it anyway. The bonus was that by spending money on posters and causes that Anita believed in, potential customers became involved – and people were drawn into the stores.

***"For The Body Shop, the environment is too important to be used simply as a marketing weapon. The Company does not believe that environmental commitment is a form of beauty contest, and unlike some companies does not wish to play on the environmental fears of its customers simply to increase the sales of products."***

*Anita Roddick.*

*"Against Animal Testing" became a very well known campaign. Anita has always believed it is wrong to test cosmetics on animals.*

*"Body Shop has a lot of feminist principles. A sense of care. Care is like the other four-letter word: love. Women are very good at it. Women bring a sense of humanity to the workplace. They are always laughing at themselves and at the powers that be."*

*From a newspaper article, February 1994.*

With two London franchises now open, publicity really picked up. Magazines carried features on Anita Roddick as a successful businesswoman and asked about the motivation behind the innovatory products The Body Shop stocked. She also began to make a series of appearances on television. There were very few women in business, and few business people who were prepared to state their views as powerfully as Anita did. "Women are more creative in their thinking," she told the business world. "They aren't usually traditionalists." "The people who are paid most are people who do not produce. They sit in front of screens moving squillions of pounds from Tokyo to New York...."

She questioned traditional business rules. Journalists found her restless energy surprising. She was reported as "rarely sitting still and quick to interrupt if she thinks people are wrong or worse, boring." Talking about herself in one interview she said: "If you are female you are supposed to be quiet and passive, speaking when you are spoken to. So if you come along with a style like mine, hooting and hollering and rushing around, it's put down to eccentricity. I play up to that." Anita's lively personality became very much a part of her and the company's success.

*The oriental style of The Body Shop headquarters at Littlehampton was a world away from the Brighton shop and garage in which Anita launched her business in 1976.*

## A company identity

By 1980, only four years after opening, the company had grown so much that Gordon decided that The Body Shop needed its own purpose-built warehouse, bottling plant, and offices. The organization was expanding at the incredible rate of two outlets a month. There were further branches in Iceland, Denmark, Finland, Holland, and Eire.

The casual way the organization had expanded in the beginning had led the Roddicks to make one big mistake. Instead of sticking to one branch style, they had offered franchise holders the choice of the traditional green, dark mahogany stain or stripped pine for the interiors. When the outlets began to look different, even though they sold the same things, Anita realized it was an error. She believed that people should be able to instantly recognize a branch of The Body Shop, or the identity of the company, wherever it was – even in different countries.

## Building an empire

Without really thinking about it, Anita Roddick had started an empire. In the first year, she had aimed to sell £15,000 worth of products to make enough money to pay the rent and feed her two children. She managed it, and three years later, the sales, or turnover, were £278,000. By 1981, it was more than fifty times as much as in the first year.

It was by now being suggested that the Roddicks should change the way they were borrowing money to continue to expand their business. Rather than borrow money from the bank – and have to pay interest – they could borrow money from ordinary people and professional investors by selling shares, or parts of the business, on the stock market.

Companies split themselves into thousands, sometimes millions, of shares and then sell them on the stock market a few at a time. All the money that people spend on buying the shares can be used by the

***"I think we're past the stage of being called a fad. Because we were different, we were still being called that while other companies came and went."***

*Anita Roddick, from* This Week *in the* Daily Express, *October 1994.*

*A range of Body Shop leaflets showing how the company's environmental message spread around the world.*

***"The Body Shop has never been just a shop. It has always been a statement, a way of saying that you are a caring customer."***

*Anita Roddick.*

*The day the Roddicks' company was floated on the stockmarket saw frantic trading in The Body Shop shares. Their share price rapidly increased throughout the day.*

company for expansion.This way, lots of people each own a small part of the business and each year, depending how big the profits made by the company are, they get a dividend payment. This is the company's way of paying the investors interest on the money they put into the company by buying the shares.

The shareholders can, at any time, sell their shares in The Body Shop to anyone else in the stock market. Sometimes the price for the shares will be higher than the amount they paid – in which case they make a profit – sometimes it is lower and they lose. It is a risk some people are prepared to make.

Changing the company from one that was owned by three people – Anita and Gordon Roddick and Ian McGlinn – into one with millions of shares which hundreds of people owned was complicated. It took two years to organize The Body Shop properly.

*Above: Share prices move up and down all the time and dealers have to react very quickly to the changes. Here, hand signals are being used to show how many shares the dealers want to buy or sell.*

## Going public

In April 1984, The Body Shop shares were offered for sale at ninety-five pence each. People thought that the business was so healthy that this price was too low so bought as many as possible. As a result the price continued to rise all day. By the end of the day shares were so popular each one was selling at £1.65.

Not all the shares were offered for sale. Ian McGlinn owned half of them and Anita and Gordon kept a large number for themselves. It was, after all, their business – they had worked to create it. When the price of all The Body Shop shares was added up the company was worth £8 million. The shares Anita and Gordon did not sell were suddenly worth £1.5 million. Without realizing it, in the eight years of hard work since founding her business, Anita Roddick, at forty-two, had become a millionaire. The

***"Nobody measures people's greatness by what they give, or how they look after the frail. It's always how much ... money have you earned? I mean is that your only vision, to have a thousand shops and X million pounds?"***

*Anita Roddick.*

***"The Body Shop would rather spend our money on good quality products and campaigning activities. ... The cosmetics industry had been peddling false dreams and downright lies which can create a high degree of unhappiness and insecurity amongst women in particular."***

*From a Body Shop advertising leaflet, May 1994.*

Roddicks were now a success. It would have been easy to sit back and enjoy their wealth but Anita and Gordon were not like that.

## For the greater good

They could have decided simply to continue to expand the business. When they sold the shares in 1984, they had thirty-eight outlets in the United Kingdom and fifty-two internationally, there were still plenty of locations for new branches. Some had already opened in eighteen countries, most in Europe, but also in Canada, Australia, Singapore and the United Arab Emirates. The target number of outlets for Japan alone was two hundred. But just being more and more successful was not going to be enough.

Both Anita and Gordon believed that they could work to make the world a better place, that it was possible to make a profit in business while behaving in a socially responsible manner.

For The Body Shop, "care for people, care for the environment and concern for animal rights" had become a central goal for the company. Anita determined to use the business to campaign for a better environment and for the rights of people to proper food, clothing and education, as well as somewhere to live and work. Being employed by The Body Shop was not just going to be a case of stocking shelves or selling bars of soap, but campaigning for the greater good.

The first task was to involve the staff and the franchise holders in campaigns. In 1985, The Body Shop teamed up with the international environmental protection group, Greenpeace, to demand an end to dumping of dangerous poisons in the North Sea.

These poisons are waste materials from factories and sewage works. Some of those companies that dumped the poisons believed they disappeared or were so diluted in the sea that they did not matter. Some do disappear, but gradually, as more and more waste is dumped into the sea, fish, plants, and animals, like porpoises and dolphins, are affected and their health threatened, or they are driven away. The company paid for one hundred giant posters on advertising hoardings. They showed a Greenpeace ship battling through stormy seas with the slogan, "Thank God Someone is Making Waves." In the corner was a little notice saying "You can join Greenpeace at The Body Shop."

It was a big step for both organizations since Greenpeace UK had never previously had links with any kind of business.

The next year the outlets themselves were used directly to campaign for an end to the slaughter of whales. This had particular significance for The Body Shop. Many of its competitors used whale oil as a basis for their cosmetics. None of The Body Shop lotions or creams used it. Instead The Body Shop used a wax similar to whale oil but it came from a desert plant, jojoba.

***"This campaign is also an opportunity for us to remind our customers that a company's success should be determined not by profit alone but also by its behaviour and amongst other things the amount of time and resources invested in environmental performance."***

*From The Body Shop's "No Time to Waste" campaign, May 1994.*

## Saving the whales

If companies used plant oil instead of whale oil it would help to save sperm whales which were fast being hunted to extinction. The numbers had dropped from more than one million to fifty

*Many cosmetic companies use spermaceti, from sperm whales, as a basis for creams. Although there are alternatives, hundreds of whales are slaughtered yearly.*

*"We have promoted ourselves through paying for the production of our window posters, the painting of the sides of our lorries, the production of T-shirts and badges. We communicate with passion and passion persuades."*
*Anita Roddick.*

thousand by the 1980s. A video on whaling was sent to all the staff so they knew what was happening. Some of the franchise holders were alarmed that Anita was getting too political. Problems with the campaign came from another direction, Greenpeace's complex organization. Anita wanted every branch to display the Save the Whale posters, but each Greenpeace group in every country had to be consulted and give its approval.

Some had doubts about linking Greenpeace with a commercial organization and only about half of The Body Shop took part. Nevertheless, The Body Shop and Greenpeace have enjoyed a long and fruitful campaigning relationship over the years.

*Left: Many groups are campaigning for a worldwide ban on the cruel practice of commercial whaling. In 1986, The Body Shop linked up with Greenpeace for a joint Save The Whale campaign.*

*Below left: Greenpeace ships spent many months patrolling the world's oceans monitoring whaling ships and pollution.*

Not all the campaigns were immediately successful either. The efforts of The Body Shop to alert the public to the problem of air pollution, where particular fumes emitted into the atmosphere combine with water in the air to fall as "acid rain," actually confused the public. This taught The Body Shop a valuable lesson in that they should keep their message simple in order to get their point across.

## Against animal testing

Such campaigns were organized centrally and then details were sent through to independent branches, with suggestions on how to communicate the message. While each franchise owner was not forced to take part, it was hoped that they would share the same beliefs and so want to join in with raising public awareness. In this way, the different franchises of The Body Shop would also present a unified image for the company as a whole.

One of the recurring campaigns that was supported by all the franchise owners was opposition to animal testing. If a supplier had tested an ingredient on animals in the last five years, The Body Shop would not buy it. Every supplier had to sign a declaration to that effect every six months and the company employed a team to ensure this was carried out. The Body Shop's policy received backing by some of the biggest animal welfare groups, such as The British Union for the Abolition of Vivisection and the International Fund for Animal Welfare.

Also, individual ingredients chosen were those that had a long history of safe human use. They were checked via a database examination to ensure there was no record of causing a negative effect. Established and new ingredients were also checked by using particular laboratory techniques. These tests showed how the ingredients behaved under certain conditions. Once it had been established that an ingredient had a safe profile, the product, that contained all the tested ingredients, could then be tried on human volunteers.

*Opposite: The Body Shop takes every opportunity to promote its environmental concerns. Here, trucks are used as mobile advertisement hoardings.*

*Below: As well as campaigning for environmental issues, The Body Shop also ran a campaign, with Amnesty International, to raise public awareness of human rights abuses around the world. Posters and leaflets were displayed in shops to explain Amnesty's work and as a result, one thousand new members joined the organization. Here Anita signs an Amnesty petition.*

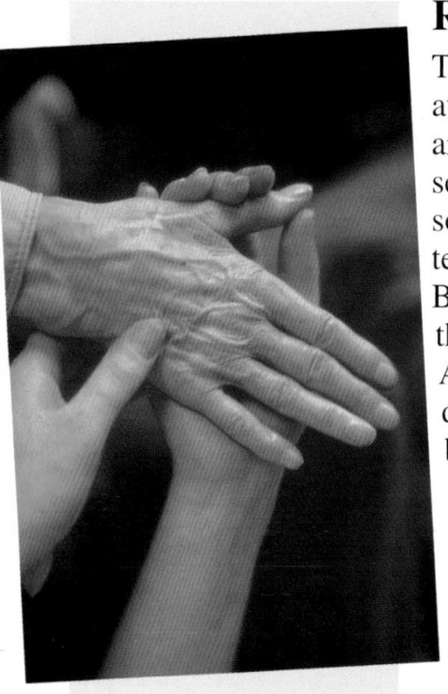

*Above and opposite: In order to give something back to the community, The Body Shop set up a Community Care Department. Working with the elderly was just one of the many different schemes that employees chose to support.*

## Real beliefs

The campaigns, such as "Against animal testing," attracted a lot of attention in the form of press articles and brought more customers into the shops to see what was going on. But Anita was criticized sometimes for using the environmental and animal testing issues as part of a publicity campaign for The Body Shop. She was accused of getting people onto the premises just as an excuse for selling products. Anita firmly believed in her principles and was determined to show that running a successful business and campaigning for social and environmental change were not mutually exclusive. She brushed aside these criticisms and carried on.

## Staff care

In 1986, the Roddicks established a training school for their staff to encompass their beliefs and underline their concern for social change as well as their product range. The idea of the training was to transmit company values, and contribute to The Body Shop vision of making the world into a better place. Within four years, there were twenty trainers and 4,844 people went through the training sessions.

Staff were given extensive training. For example, when a new herbal hair tinting range was introduced, courses were organized on which product suited which type of hair, where each dye came from, and what it contained. Staff were told how to advise customers to put it on and even how to solve disasters if hair did not turn out to be the desired tint. Correct training makes everyone feel part of a team and the customer feels cared for.

Additionally, every employee was given the oportunity to spend half a day a month working in one of the hundreds of community projects round the world that the company supported. The staff were not just selling hair and skin products, they were pushing for social change. It proved to be a great motivator and made people proud to work for The Body Shop. As a result, this improved their performance for the company.

## "Pinstriped dinosaurs"

Some criticisms were made against The Body Shop, saying that it forced its views on its employees and tried to make them crusaders. A small number of staff left, but the success of the organization was, in a large part, due to the positive and enthusiastic attitude of the staff. Staff were issued with red envelopes so that if they had suggestions, or complaints, they could bypass the normal chain of command and communicate directly with Anita or Gordon. Staff were encouraged to feel that they could contribute to the running of both their outlet and the company as a whole. Suggestion boxes became standard to every branch.

Whether financial advisers or accountants understood what was going on Anita doubted. She certainly had a low opinion of them and once called city business people "pinstriped dinosaurs" because they were only interested in how much profit a company made. Rather than discuss the profits,

***"The Body Shop is not simply a manufacturer or retailer of toiletries and cosmetics. We actively attempt to minimise our impact on the environment; we promote fair trading relationships; we are against animal testing in the cosmetics industry; and we encourage education, awareness and involvement among staff and customers."***

*From The Body Shop Company Profile, May 1994.*

Anita wanted to know how The Body Shop rated in terms of education, caring for the staff, on the quirkiness scale and whether it was fulfilling its social responsibilities.

The "dinosaurs," however, need not have worried about profits. Odd though The Body Shop business methods might have seemed to them, profits improved in leaps and bounds and kept on rising steadily through the next five years.

## Education

Although environmental campaigning was important to Anita, she began to look for new areas in which she could develop the business. Other businesses were operating which had similar ideas to the Roddicks – instead of just making a profit they put some of their resources and time into campaigns they believed in. For example, an American ice cream company, Ben and Jerry's, put 7.5% of its profits into helping the poor and homeless.

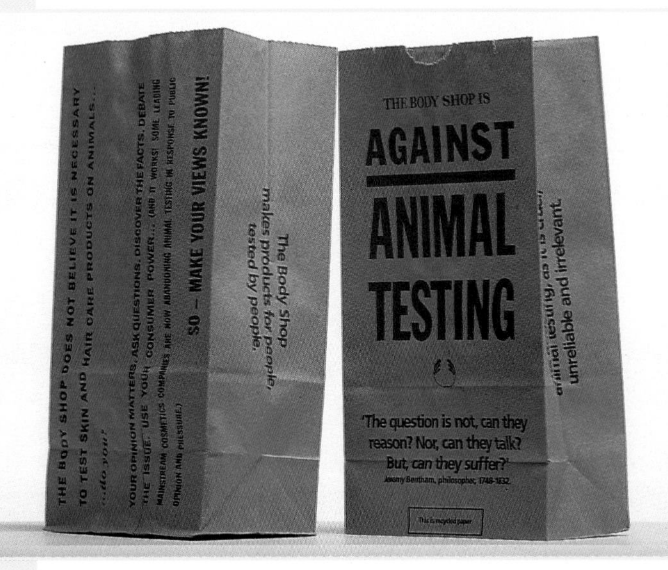


*Another way the company raises public awareness. Here, bags are used to highlight The Body Shop's beliefs and concerns. The company has always shunned fancy packaging.*

While Anita was exploring these areas Gordon continued to run the administration of the business. Anita introduced him to her contacts in the United States and the group held regular meetings to discuss

*Above: For the "Stop the Burning" campaign in May 1989, Anita and 250 of The Body Shop staff arrived at the Brazilian Embassy in London with sack loads of letters protesting against the destruction of the South American rainforests.*

*Left: Writing letters is one of the many ways The Body Shop has raised awareness for its campaigns.*

how they could use their businesses to help communities. One of the views they all shared was that education was vital to running a successful business. This did not mean just the employees and the customers, but also the "pinstriped dinosaurs."

As a result, Anita also tried to educate the shareholders. Every year the shareholders were invited to a meeting to hear a report on the company's progress and profits. They were also given an account of the education of staff, the campaigns against animal testing, and the efforts to save the environment by the staff and the company. Anita also used it as an opportunity to tell the shareholders what her environment and community plans for the next year were and made it clear that The Body Shop was not just a way of making profits.

*The Body Shop linked up with Friends of the Earth for campaigns to stop acid rain and to protect the ozone layer.*

## Environmental awareness

Part of the campaign to promote the interest and involvement of staff and shareholders meant the formation of an environmental projects department. This was designed to make sure that the company did its best to help the environment by cutting waste and by trying to reduce energy consumption. Materials which came from threatened species or threatened environments were not to be used on The Body Shop premises or in its products. In addition, products should not involve cruelty to animals, and the company's activities should not adversely affect other countries, especially poor countries. This was setting high standards but Anita wanted to go further. She wanted to establish links with national and international environmental groups and encourage outlets, franchise holders, and the staff to get involved in projects in their areas.

## Force for change

As the number of customers per week started to run into millions, and the numbers passing the shop windows many times more, Anita and Gordon Roddick realized that there was now a huge potential to become a force for change. They had always been passionate social campaigners and believed that business was about more than making money. Here was an opportunity to behave in a socially responsible manner and use the influence The Body Shop was gaining to become a powerful force for change.

From then on campaigns became a regular feature of the shops: from global issues, such as acid rain, recycling and whales, to such local issues as cleaning up hedgerows and ponds. As well as working with Greenpeace, links were established with campaigning organizations like Friends of the Earth, and Amnesty International. Amnesty campaigns against the violation of human rights around the world, for example imprisonment without trial, torture and capital punishment.

It wasn't just about campaigning either. As the company grew, so did its knowledge and expertise. Staff both in the shops and at Head Office were encouraged to be aware of their own impact on the environment. Paper was collected and reused or recycled and before long an environmental department was established in the company to monitor and, where necessary, improve its environmental performance. Company trucks became mobile advertisement hoardings for The Body Shop campaigns with "Reuse, Refill, Recycle" written in huge letters. Bags given to customers carried stories of Amazonian Indians whose land and lifestyle were under threat.

***"We are different from most other retailers. We are not looking for 100 per cent education standards. We are looking for commitment, for enthusiasm, for a loyalty and for an empathy for our beliefs and the way we do things."***

*Anita Roddick.*

*"ONCE IS NOT ENOUGH" – another poster used in The Body Shop's recycling campaign to encourage customers to return their bottles for refilling.*

## Having fun

The campaigns were supported by franchisees across the world. Sometimes there were questions about whether it was right for the company to campaign, for example, against the Gulf War, and staff at all levels were given the opportunity to express their views and concerns. There were also times when campaigns threatened to get in the way of business. As shops became more enthusiastic about campaigning, collection tins and petitions began to proliferate. It was all part of the learning process about how to combine social concerns with a profitable business.

***"Her belief is that business must make human values as important a criterion of successful management as profit."***

*Maggie Drummond, from* The Daily Telegraph, *November 14, 1991.*

*Appalled at the conditions in Romanian orphanages after the collapse of the Ceaucescu government, Anita was determined to take action. Here, one of The Body Shop's many volunteers comforts an orphaned baby.*

Anita believed that the success of the business was partly based on the fact that she was passionate about her beliefs and the staff shared her enthusiasm. The enthusiasm was infectious and the customers found The Body Shop an exciting place to visit.

Anita was having fun and so were the staff. They enjoyed their jobs and they worked in the opposite direction to everyone else. In the 1980s, greed was fashionable, success was measured by excess. The Body Shop was preaching the opposite, and by doing so it was breaking all the rules. It was talking about campaigning, education, social and environmental issues. But this was still not a common way of doing business and there was a long way to go before other companies accepted that success and social responsibility could go hand in hand.

## Adopting orphans

In 1990, when a scandal of babies abandoned in Romania was world news, Anita visited a village orphanage called Halaucesti. Appalled by the state of the children – unwashed, sometimes unclothed, hungry, sick, and without any kind of education or stimulus – she determined to do something. She made an appeal for The Body Shop volunteers to go. Within six weeks the project to renovate the orphanage had begun. Sixty volunteers made a long-term commitment to the welfare of the children.

Another campaign involved working with Amnesty International and Greenpeace to draw attention to the plight of political prisoners and endangered peoples in Nigeria. Oil was discovered in Nigeria in the 1950s. It was on the land of the Ogoni – a small tribe of four hundred thousand to five hundred thousand people. They were a farming and fishing community who were able to produce enough food for themselves and many others in the Rivers State of Nigeria. Oil became the dominant product in the Nigerian economy. The Ogoni enjoyed little benefit from the huge wealth found on their land. In fact because of spills from oil wells their land was ruined and they had to import food. The Ogoni leader, Ken Saro-Wiwa, made his views plain to the rest of the world, but was thrown in prison by the military government. The Body Shop and Greenpeace drew the world's attention to this appalling situation, and alongside Amnesty International have continually tried to help the Movement for the Survival of the Ogoni People – MOSOP. In the 1990s, they worked with MOSOP in its fight to prevent further destruction of the land.

The Body Shop, Greenpeace and Amnesty International were also ahead of many nations in recognizing that Ken Saro-Wiwa was in danger from the military government. They joined in the campaign to try to secure his freedom. Unfortunately this was to no avail. The Nigerian government became increasingly desperate to silence any voices of protest against it and executed Saro-Wiwa in November 1995. Much of the world was united in disgust at this action.

***"Her most often preached sermon runs as follows. It is no use pouring aid in to Third World countries; it will just evaporate in the deserts and jungles. What they need is trade and the exchange of exotic natural products for Western currency."***

*Maggie Drummond, from* The Daily Telegraph, *November 14, 1991.*

*A customer signs The Body Shop's petition protesting at the destruction of the Brazilian rainforest.*

*These lush, green rainforests are important for us all. They provide a home and a livelihood for many Indian tribes. They also have a huge effect on the world's climate. It is vital to conserve them.*

## "No time to waste"

In Hong Kong, pupils aged ten to fifteen years were encouraged to carry out environmental audits of their schools under the slogan "No Time to Waste." The slogan was a part of the information packs put together by The Body Shop.

Anita began to use her wealth and influence on other projects. £2.5 million was invested personally into making a television documentary about tribal peoples. The message was that Western civilization could learn a lot from the tribal lifestyles rather than standing back as they disappear.

Rainforests contain almost half of the world's known flora and fauna species, and at least a quarter of known medicines are from the forests. They

Felled trunks of majestic slow growing hardwood rainforest trees. They will never be replaced.

contain plants that cure malaria, treatments for epilepsy, blood cancer and possibly AIDS. In the 1990s, more than 140 million people lived in or around tropical rainforests, yet about fifty-three acres of rainforest were being destroyed every minute and ninety tribes were thought to have disappeared in the Amazon forests of Brazil during the twentieth century. Making people aware of this was part of Anita Roddick's continuing attempt to bring the plight of distant tribes to the attention of the world.

**"For The Body Shop, care for people, care for the environment and concern for animal rights are essential components in its business strategy. This requires a dynamic relationship between the Company, its staff and its customers."**

*David Wheeler, Body Shop International – No Time to Waste.*

## Trading with communities in need

The purpose of giving aid to poor countries changed dramatically between 1960 and 1990. Simply giving money or food was no longer seen as helpful, except in the case of famine relief. When people are starving then food aid must be the first priority, but this was not seen as a long-term answer anymore.

Once the famine was over, the survivors needed to be provided with seed to plant new crops for the next season to prevent it happening again. They should then get further help to prevent famine recurring, for example by planting trees. When trees are chopped down in vast numbers, the protective canopy that they provide is removed. The top layer of soil is then easily washed away, or eroded, when the rains come. Planting trees retains the moisture, keeps the soil fertile, and prevents soil erosion.

The slogan "Trade Not Aid" was a further development of the principle of practical help, an effort to enable tribal groups to be self supporting. It was based on the simple principle that if countries traded fairly, aid wouldn't be so heavily relied upon. Most communities make products that are sold in their locality or bartered in exchange for other products. When westerners arrive with their ideas of a consumer society, they disturb this trading pattern. Local products are bought up in large quantities, at a price that seems cheap to westerners, and they then sell them on to retailers at high prices, often twenty or thirty times what they paid, making a huge profit out of the tribes.

## International links

There are many disputes about how best to help these traditional peoples. Some feel that the villages and people should be protected against western influences so that they can continue their lifestyle undisturbed. Others, like Anita Roddick, believed that it was impossible to keep the modern world back, but that the tribes people should be put in a position of strength and not taken advantage of by westerners. Anita made it part of her company's policy that her business should respect other cultures, that the tribespeople should benefit from any trading, and that their ideas and products should be credited directly to themselves.

The Body Shop now has solid links with a number

*Above: Instead of attending "boring old trade fairs," Anita set up direct relations with local traders and crafts people in developing countries. Here she is enjoying bartering in a Ghanaian market.*

*Left: Sisal being held up for inspection in Mexico. Sisal is like rope and comes from a tropical plant. The Body Shop used it to make body scrubs. This is an example of a successful "Trade Not Aid" scheme.*

of producer groups worldwide, providing direct and indirect employment for thousands of people. The Body Shop works with cooperatives, family businesses and with tribal councils. By 1995, there were links with producer groups in Nepal, India, Brazil, Mexico, Russia, Nicaragua, Bangladesh, Ghana, Zambia and the USA. These trade links may also result in more benefits, such as provision of health care, education and other advantages for the wider communities involved.

***"Trade Not Aid is quickly growing into a cornerstone for The Body Shop. It provides a platform from which our purchasing power is used to direct money straight to the primary producers. The next ten years will see a huge development in this part of the business not least because it does not patronise or degrade the people with whom we trade."***

*Gordon Roddick, from a "Trade Not Aid" fact sheet.*

## First try fails

Despite its success, finding projects to support in the first place was more difficult. The Body Shop's first scheme involved making round wooden rollers for massaging feet. The "footsie rollers" project in the province of Tamil Nadu in southern India seemed the perfect scheme. More than half the forty million inhabitants of the province were very poor and there were also many destitute children. An organization, called the Boys' Town Trust, was providing homes for some of these children, giving them an education and teaching them a trade so that when they grew up they could earn a living.

The Body Shop decided to sponsor eighty-five boys to live in its own Boys' Town built with money from franchise holders. When Gordon and Anita visited it in 1988, the boys were already installed. Anita was entranced by it all and it was many months before she realized that things had gone wrong. "I am always ready to put my faith in people and I am rarely burned. When I am, it hurts – and it never hurt more than when I discovered our first Trade Not Aid project had gone terribly wrong."

When she discovered that the footsie rollers were not being made by the boys at all, but by low paid people working in terrible conditions she felt shocked and betrayed. The Body Shop, which had been paying 20% of its profits from the venture into a special fund for the Boys' Town broke its links with the project. But this did not dampen Anita's desire to make a project work in India. In the 1990s, a successful project trading

*Opposite top: On a trip to Kenya, Anita Roddick is stunned by the beauty of these Masai women and their intricate necklaces. They seem equally fascinated by her long hair.*

in wooden products was once again thriving in Tamil Nadu.

In the meantime, Anita looked for other projects and made a link with the Kayapo Indians in the eastern Amazon in Brazil.

## The value of oil

The Indians' way of life in the Amazon is threatened by continued burning and logging of the forest trees. Gold and diamond miners used chemicals, including mercury, in the rivers which poisoned both fish and people using the rivers for water supplies. The only way that the Indians themselves can see to save their forest is to find a form of income that does not itself destroy the home in which they live. In conjunction with Anita, the idea was developed that a freely available and renewable resource might be the key.

*Above: Anita and a Woodabe medicine man swap beauty tips in the Sahara Desert during a fact-finding mission in 1990.*

With the help of simple technology provided by The Body Shop, the Kayapo produced Brazil nut oil themselves, for use in hair conditioner sold throughout the world. The oil fetched a far higher price than the whole nuts would have and all the profits were kept to pay for health, education and other needs identified by the Indians themselves.

***"We live in a society that makes no value at all of anything south of the equator and I was brought up to think science and technology was the answer. But while we talk about responsible citizenship, these tribes live it."***

Anita Roddick, *from* The Sunday Times, June 28,1992.

*Opposite top: Watching local women grind nuts to make shea butter in Ghana. Anita believed that it was possible for large companies to trade fairly with underdeveloped countries without destroying their cultures.*

*Opposite bottom: Anita tries an age-old beauty treatment in Columbia.*

## Body scrub

Anita repeatedly flew round the world visiting countries. She hoped very much to find ways to trade for mutual benefit. In Mexico, the company bought body scrub mitts made from cactus. In the United States, The Body Shop traded with the Santa Ana Pueblo Indians in blue corn for use in a range of products; in Nepal, a trade in handmade paper products allowed profits to be used to support education and healthcare projects.

The Body Shop did its best to publicize these trade links, and to persuade other companies to go in for similar schemes. Some organizations, however, did not agree with these methods. They believed that trading with money, as opposed to the bartering system changes the complexion of the whole local society.

With cash, the Indians could buy western medicines, radios, clothes and watches, but this might mean that the traditional medicines and the local culture could die out. However, The Body Shop and many other organizations felt strongly that it was helping these communities move toward financial and social independence. While its fair trade schemes made up only a small amount of its overall profit, it was a growing part of its business plans.

*Below: Like mothers everywhere, Anita loved discussing children, and was obviously smitten with this Kyapo baby.*

## Getting the idea

By 1994, Anita had been spending between four to five months a year overseas. She visited The Body Shop projects with such communities as the Kayapo Indians, and she

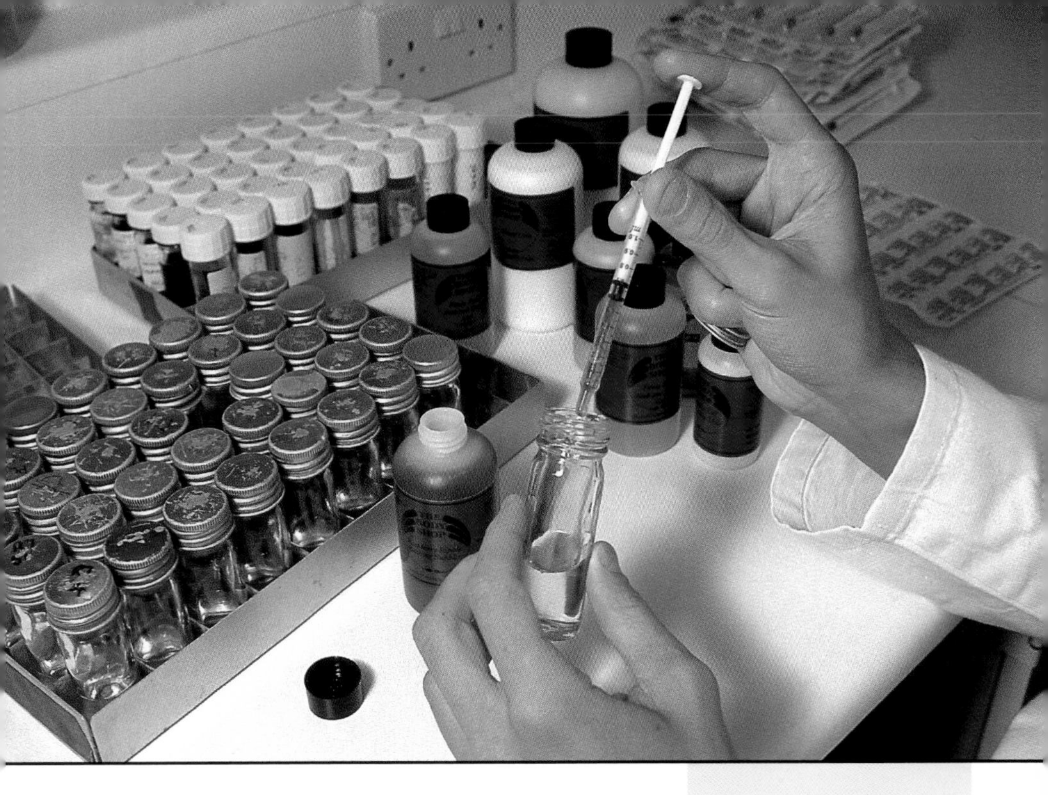


collected ideas for new products.

All the while Anita Roddick pushed forward The Body Shop principles worldwide.

Many of Anita's ideas were generated by her trips to meet the different communities with which she dealt – she listened to their traditional remedies and recipes. On her return, she passed variations of these ideas onto the chemists who worked in the company's laboratories. The chemists assessed each idea, testing the ingredients involved. Because many used natural ingredients, such as bananas, they had to ensure that the mixture wouldn't "go off." Once all the ingredients were mixed together, they had to make sure the new concoction would pollute the environment as little as possible – and it would look, and smell, good.

Once a few variations of the new product had been carefully tested in the laboratory, they could be tested on the human volunteers. The product tester then assessed how the product performed. The results were passed back to the laboratory, where

*Above: A company chemist conducts one of the many quality control processes that The Body Shop products have to go through before finally being distributed.*

*Opposite top: Maintaining strict hygiene levels is one important part of the production process at The Body Shop.*

*Opposite bottom: Fixing labels to recyclable and refillable bottles before distribution to The Body Shops worldwide.*

each new product was reviewed. Nine out of ten products would not go beyond this stage – they might not look right, smell right, or they might be too complicated or expensive to produce, or they might not do the thing they are supposed to do, such as moisturize or cleanse.

After a product had been given the go-ahead, production could start. The ingredients had to be bought-in in bulk and the factory machines set up for specialized production – each product usually required a slightly different approach. Cleanliness and hygiene were of the utmost importance. Much of the production of the mixture was computerized – the computer checking the weight of each ingredient, controlling the water levels and temperature throughout the process.

The finished mixture would be transferred into pallecons, large, sealed, waterproof bags, and transported to the bottling plant.

***"Together with the educational and campaigning activities which the company promotes, The Body Shop hopes to provide an example of how a practical and honest commitment to the environment can coexist with successful retailing and customer support."***

*Sally Power, The Body Shop International.*

## Helping the environment

The Body Shop headquarters offered a tour in order for the public to see the different stages of this process. A constant stream of visitors looked at the offices, factory, warehouse, laboratories, and crèche. Electric cars took tourists round.

These special cars ran on batteries charged by The Body Shop's own wind generator. This generator also provided power for a visitors' area.

While most companies undertook research and development into new products alone, The Body Shop looked at new ways of recycling and reducing waste. It was willing to experiment with new materials and to re-use old ones. The waste products from the factory – although cut to a minimum – still required a discharge into the sewage system. A greenhouse containing a series of different plants to filter the waste through was built. The idea was to get the plants to "eat" the effluent. This would mean that the amount of waste discharged to the sewer could be further reduced.

In Anita's attempt to reduce the use of nuclear power and carbon dioxide emissions, the waste gas

***"How can you be wrong when you borrow ideas from Mahatma Gandhi, from Martin Luther King, from Chief Seattle? I go around the world looking for people whose vision is clearer than my own and I bow down before them."***

*Anita Roddick, from* The Guardian, September 11, 1991.

from burning coal, oil and other fossil fuels, she strongly supported renewable energy. Wind and water can be used over and over again and do not create any poisonous waste products. Anita promoted the use of wind farms with twenty to twenty-four turbines to provide the energy needed to run the company's headquarters and outlets within Britain. The aim was that this source should provide enough power to match the amount used by The Body Shop for ten years. In 1993, the company took a stake in a wind farm project in Wales. Energy-use in Body Shops in Britain was cut by 10% in two years. The Body Shop headquarters in Watersmead, Littlehampton, in a green roofed pagoda, were designed to take advantage of the sunshine and make the most of thermal heating, as well as providing a good place to work. By 1995, the headquarters were 30% more energy efficient than two years before.

*The Body Shop Child Development Centre opened at Head Office in January 1990 to provide a fun and safe environment for the children of employees. The Body Shop believes affordable child care should be made available to all parents who wish to work.*

## Not quite as rich

Although The Body Shop continued to expand, and Anita and Gordon were thinking of new schemes to advance their ideas, there were setbacks. The Body Shop was not immune from what happened in the rest of the business world.

In 1992, a worldwide recession damaged businesses, and some companies had to close down. The Body Shop suffered, too. For the first time since the business began, sales in Britain dropped slightly. Profits were not going to be as large as Gordon Roddick had hoped. This affected the shares that people held in the company. They had gone up and down many times over the years, but this time they dropped considerably. The value of the whole business, therefore, was reduced. There was then less money available to be devoted to opening new stores and to buying more stock.

However, all the branches were still trading, everyone had their jobs. The company was still expanding, too. In that year seventy-three new outlets had already opened and the company expected another sixty to open by the end of the year.

*A rare moment of relaxation for the Roddicks in their hectic schedule. Gordon has said of Anita, "I've been trying to get her to slow down for 25 years."*

***"What The Body Shop is good at is its communications within the business, its products, its social activities and its market. People are told to speak up and make their views heard. Ideas for improving the business are eagerly sought."***

*Bob Reynolds, from* The 100 Best Companies to work for in the UK.

## A testing time

By the beginning of 1994, the company had passed the milestone of more than one thousand shops, and people were beginning to wonder if there was any limit to the expansion of The Body Shop chain.

However, people were waiting for even the tiniest opportunity to find any inconsistencies between the high standards The Body Shop claimed to have and what they saw as "reality." In September 1994, The Body Shop suddenly found itself the target of a stinging attack in a small, limited-circulation American magazine, *Business Ethics.* The criticism made the headlines on the radio, television and front pages of newspapers. Gordon Roddick tried to minimize the damage – "The Company does not pretend to be perfect or to have all the answers. However, the Company does believe that through its staff and customers, positive choices can be exercised which help minimize environmental impacts in the production and use of skin and hair care products."

## The unfair attack

The Body Shop shares dropped dramatically on the Stock Exchange. Some share-buying companies, called ethical investment funds, that had invested in The Body Shop because of its green image, threatened to withdraw their support. Anita Roddick and her company fought back and issued a detailed statement refuting the allegations.

Later, when challenged, Anita Roddick put it just as boldly – "Our products combine traditional wisdom, ancient herbal remedies and modern scientific research, using ingredients with a long history of safe human use.... Although fair trade is currently only a small part of what we do we are committed to developing such relationships with communities in need around the world." This was just what her supporters wanted to hear. Peter Webster of Ethical Investment Research made it clear what the real case was – "The Body Shop do a number of things which truly make them different from other companies. They may not always achieve everything they hope to do – but that's no excuse for companies not to aim high ... It is wrong to measure The Body Shop against perfection, because no company is perfect. It is far more valid to compare them with other companies."

## Forever green

Independent investigations were launched into the allegations. Based on these findings the ethical investment funds in the United States and Britain decided that The Body Shop still met the best standards. They decided to continue their support. For its part, The Body Shop pledged to continue to be completely open about its claims about its green image. The Roddicks promised to increase the amount of ingredients bought on fair trade principles. Profits were put back into the company to address the issues that executives of The Body Shop held dear. Product research and development was given an even higher profile. The Body Shop share price recovered.

***"Broadly speaking, The Body Shop has been unfairly criticised. A number of claims made in headlines have turned out to be untrue, or at least misleading. Body Shop have been compared with perfection, rather than other companies. The practical question for both ethical investors and consumers remains 'If not Body Shop, then who?'"***

*EIRIS Research into criticism of The Body Shop.*

## A campaigning spirit

Anita and Gordon Roddick were just as determined as ever that they should continue to assist social change. Through The Body Shop, they concentrated on new campaigns – one being to support the women's movement. They sponsored a number of women's groups in an effort to unite their cause to improve women's pay, childcare facilities and access to training. Their commitment to such policies was reflected in their own facilities for employees at their headquarters. In January 1990, a purpose-built crèche for children ranging from the ages of three months to five years in the nursery, and five to eleven years in the after school scheme had been opened.

Added to this was The Body Shop's determination to campaign against violence to women. In 1994, The Body Shop joined forces with American Express to provide £75,000 to fund an initiative in the south of Britain against such violence.

***"Since she opened her first shop in Brighton in 1976, 48-year-old Roddick has done more than simply fill the world's bathrooms with plastic bottles of sweetie-coloured unguents. As well as flogging the soap, she has climbed up on the soapbox, to preach passionately about human rights and the environment."***

*Kate Saunders, from* The Sunday Times, Sept 1, 1991.

> ***"You can fly the flag of social change and still make a profit."***
>
> *Anita Roddick.*

> ***"By the end of this century any company not operating like The Body Shop will have a hard time operating at all. Personally, I don't know how ... anybody can survive running a successful business in the Nineties without caring."***
>
> *Anita Roddick, from a magazine article, 1992.*

> ***"I think The Body Shop can be a role model for other companies. We've brought in a feminine language. We talk about love. We talk about care. We'd rather close down than test our products on animals."***
>
> *Anita Roddick.*

## Multi-millionaire

Back in 1976, no one would have believed it, least of all Anita Roddick, that less than twenty years later there would be branches of The Body Shop all over the world from the Arctic to Australia. By 1990, with more than one thousand staff working at the headquarters in Littlehampton, The Body Shop had become an internationally-known name with stores in forty-five countries. By April 1995, there were 1,300 outlets trading over four hundred products in twenty different languages, employing more than seven thousand people.

It had become policy that each outlet should sell the same products, in the same style packaging, recognizable from the original shop in Brighton. Inside, the damp was no longer part of the decor, but the green paint was the same, along with the big posters and the simple messages.

Anita Roddick had become probably the best known businesswoman in the world and one of the most talked about. She had also become a multi-millionaire. More than anything else it was her personality, her reputation as a self-confessed "mega-mouth," coupled with the back-up of her husband, Gordon, that had led to the extraordinary success of the business.

## Awards and recognition

In the 1990s, Anita continued to travel the world lecturing and, as she put it, hectoring, other businesses to change the way they worked. However, through The Body Shop's campaigning and bid to uphold ethics as well as profits, the company has sometimes laid itself open to criticism. Despite this she and her company managed to make a tremendous impact on environmental issues and on industry.

In recognition of this, she was showered with awards, receiving three environmental prizes in 1993 alone, two from Mexico and one from Australia. But it was not just for her environmental work. In five years, she received five honorary degrees from universities and colleges, and business awards from

*A universal symbol of success - the popping of champagne corks, as Anita celebrates being named Businesswoman of the Year for 1986.*

Britain, the United States, and Finland, as well as recognition for voluntary work done by staff.

In *The Body Shop Book,* Anita compared her business philosophy to that of other cosmetics companies: "The interweaving of profit and principle is, I believe, the major point of difference between The Body Shop and other cosmetics companies. It's the guiding light of every aspect of our business, from the way we find our ingredients to the volunteer work done by our staff in their communities all around the world. I'm not fool enough to believe you can change the world with a new face cream, but you *can* do something with the money that accrues from the sale of that face cream."

The world of business will never be quite the way it was before The Body Shop. In the 1980s and beginning of the 1990s, when profit seemed to

*Anita could never have dreamt that The Body Shop would be so successful when she launched her first shop. By the mid-1990s, there were 1300 outlets in 46 countries, trading in 23 languages.*

be the only thing that mattered, Anita Roddick preached the opposite. The staff were important, the products and what they contained were important, the environment was important, the campaigns for tribal peoples, for fair trade, were important.

By being so outspoken she broke all the business rules, but that did not stop The Body Shop organization making profits and growing. The Body Shop has had its critics who say that the good-hearted image was just to draw in more customers in order to sell more products, but that does not explain why Anita and Gordon Roddick continued to work so hard.

In the second half of the 1990s, Anita Roddick still believed in The Body Shop as a force for change, and not just an expanding money-making enterprise. She was often criticized, but she hoped her business style could lead business onto better things. "We believe at The Body Shop that it is possible to hand on the planet to our children in a better state than we found it and with a fairer system of wealth distribution," Anita told the business world. "To play our part in that brighter future is our main goal."

***"I'm convinced their heart's in the right place. I feel The Body Shop has helped to show that it is possible for business to be concerned about the community and to be profitable. That's the major contribution The Body Shop has made.***

*Ben Cohen, 1994.*

## Important dates

1942 Anita Perella is born to Gilda and Donny Perella in Littlehampton, England.

1950 Anita's parents are divorced. Uncle Henry, Anita's real father, returns from living in America to marry Gilda.

1962 Anita Perella, aged twenty, goes to Israel for three months work on a kibbutz and begins to travel.

1963 Anita Perella finds work in France, Greece and Switzerland.

1964 Anita Perella visits the South Pacific, Tahiti, and Australia. She is then arrested in South Africa and deported for breaking apartheid rules. On her return to England she meets Gordon Roddick.

1969 August: the Roddicks' first daughter, Justine, is born.

1970 Anita Perella and Gordon Roddick are married.

1971 July: The Roddicks' second daughter, Samantha, is born.

1976 March 27: Anita Roddick opens her first Body Shop at 22 Kensington Gardens, Brighton, England.
September: the second Body Shop outlet opens at Chichester, England.

1977 Gordon Roddick returns from his travels and takes over the bottling and label making side of the business.

1978 The first independently-owned branches of The Body Shop open in England and in Brussels, Belgium.

1979 The first branches of The Body Shop open in Stockholm in Sweden and Athens in Greece.

1982 October: The Body Shop moves into new warehouses and offices in Littlehampton. New Body Shop outlets open in Iceland, Denmark, Finland, Holland and Eire.

1984 April: Body Shop shares go onto the market in the UK Stock Exchange and reach the value of £8 million. Gordon and Anita are each worth £1.5 million.

1985 The Body Shop teams up with Greenpeace on an advertising campaign against dumping dangerous poisons in the North Sea.

1986 The Body Shop launches a Save the Whale Campaign with Greenpeace.
The Body Shop launches a training school for all its staff.
The Body Shop forms an Environmental Projects Department to ensure that the company is doing its best to help the environment and to

establish links with other international environmental groups.
Anita Roddick is named UK Businesswoman of the Year.

1988 The Body Shop establishes its own Boys Town in South India, providing education and homes for eighty-five boys.
July1: The Body Shop opens a store in New York, the first in the USA.

1990 May: Anita Roddick travels to the Romanian village of Halaucesti to visit orphaned children.
July: The Body Shop launches its Romanian Relief Project to renovate and begin long-term care for the orphaned children.

1993 Anita Roddick receives three prizes in recognition of her work for the environment.

1994 September: The Body Shop finds itself the target of criticism after an article appears in an American Magazine questioning The Body Shop's ethics.

1994 The Body Shop joins forces with American Express to campaign against violence to women.

1995 The Body Shop has 1,300 outlets worldwide, selling more than four hundred products and employing more than seven thousand people.

# Glossary

**Acid rain:** Rain that has been polluted by chemicals and released into the atmosphere by burning coal or oil.

**Administration:** The management of the concerns or affairs of a business.

**Apartheid:** A political policy that organizes society to keep different races apart in schools, hotels, restaurants, beaches and even on public transport. In South Africa it meant the dominance by the white minority.

**Audit:** A thorough inspection or examination of the accounts, or finances, of a business.

**Campaign:** A series of activities, such as rallies, posters, broadcasts and advertisements, that are aimed at achieving a certain political or social goal.

**Collateral:** Money or property which is used as a guarantee that someone will repay a loan.

**Commercial:** When something is commercial, the intention is to sell goods to make a *profit.*

**Commodity:** One of the goods that is a *commercial* item to be sold to make a *profit.*

**Consumer:** Someone who buys goods for their own needs.

**Database:** A store of information organized on a computer.

**Doctrine:** The principles, or ideas held to or believed in by a person or a group of people.

**Entrepreneur:** A person with a sharp *commercial* sense who is prepared to take risks in setting up a new business with a view to making a *profit.*

**Environment:** All the surroundings – people, things, events and countryside – around an area that affect the life of those living there.

**Franchise:** The right or permission given or sold to a retailer by a manufacturing company to market their products.

**Hoardings:** Large boards used for displaying advertising posters.

**Holistic:** The treatment of the whole person, mental as well as physical, rather than just the symptoms of a complaint.

**Interest:** A charge made on money that is borrowed.

**Kibbutz:** A communal settlement, such as a farm or factory, in Israel, where the workers live together and share all the duties and income.

**Manufacture:** To produce goods on a large scale, usually involving machinery.

**Marketing:** Presenting your products attractively in a *campaign* to sell them.

**Outlet:** A *commercial* organization that retails the goods of a certain company.

**Ozone layer:** A fragile layer of gas, twelve to thirty miles (20-50 kms) above the earth's surface, made from the oxygen-related ozone. It creates a protective layer, filtering the sun's ultraviolet rays before they reach the earth.

**Product:** An item that is *manufactured* for sale.

**Promotion:** To encourage the sale of a *product,* often by advertising.

**Profit:** The amount of money gained in business or *trade,* when an item is sold for more than it cost to produce.

**Publicity:** A way of attracting public attention to something, in this case, a *product.*

**Raw materials:** The basic materials used to make a *product* before they undergo *manufacturing* processes.

**Recycling:** To process used material, such as paper or bottles, so that it can be used again.

**Retail:** The sale of goods, usually in shops, to *consumers.*

**Share:** A part of a company's capital, or disposable money, that can be bought and owned by a member of the company or the public. If a person buys a share, he or she is then entitled to a percentage of the company's profits.

**Sponsor:** A person or organization that supports or pays for another person to be able to do something.

**Stock Exchange:** The place where shares in different companies are bought and sold.

**Trade:** To buy and sell goods or *products.*

**Venture:** An arrangement for buying and selling goods where there may be a risk of loss as well as gain.

**Vivisection:** The procedure of experimenting on live animals for scientific purposes.

# Index